Knowing Yourself

Enhancing Communication

The Business Leader Series

Fiona Campbell

Copyright © 2014 Fiona Campbell

All rights reserved. No part of this publication can be reproduced or transmitted in any form or by any means without permission in writing from Fiona Campbell

ISBN-10:1496137302
ISBN-13:978-1496137302

Table Of Contents

Introduction	1
The Qualities Of A Business Leader	5
We Live In Two Worlds	9
The R.A.F.T. Model©	15
Keeping Your Leadership Styles Clean	23
Creating A Leadership Mindset	29
Using Intention To Reduce Meeting Times	33
Verbal and non-verbal communication	41
Leading Others	47
Knowing yourself	51
Roundup	53

Introduction

"Management is about arranging and telling. Leadership is about nurturing and enhancing." **Tom Peters**

Welcome to Knowing Yourself - Enhancing Communication - The Business Leaders Series.

I am Fiona Campbell, an Executive Coach, and an NLP Business Coach Trainer, and I coach and train people to enhance their communication and leadership skills.

This book has evolved from the leadership development programmes I have been delivering since 1993.

If you want to lead people more effectively, improve your existing leadership skills, better understand how you come across to others, create a more powerful leadership presence, progress in your career or are looking to become a business leader, then this book is for you.

Each chapter in this book includes actionable skills, where you do an exercise on the topic covered in that particular chapter.

It is only by doing something that we learn it. If you want to get to know yourself better as a business leader, I highly recommend you do the exercises. Most of these actionable skills are easily transferred to your workplace. To get maximum value from this book use a workbook or journal to track your progress.

Successful leaders know the value of having the flexibility to stay one step ahead of the people they lead.

They have the vision to see the big picture of where they are going, along with foresight and attention to detail. They spot the challenges that could (and often do) occur, and find ways to overcome these challenges before they get out of hand.

Great leaders are highly perceptive. They know their own capabilities, strengths and weaknesses. They know the people they lead well, and utilise the individual strengths within their team, to achieve the best outcome. They communicate clearly and concisely with everyone, to keep them motivated and focused on their goals and objectives.

True leaders assume personal responsibility, both for their own actions and those of their team. People want to follow them, whether they have a job title of leader or not.

So, if you are ready to learn more about what it takes to lead others well, get to know yourself better as a leader and enhance your communication skills - lets get started.

The Qualities Of A Business Leader

"A leader is best when people barely know he exists, when his work is done, his aim fulfilled, they will say: we did it ourselves" **Lao Tzu**

A leader is someone who has followers who look to them for guidance.

They have the vision, drive and determination and take personal responsibility to lead a task or project to a conclusion. They identify goals to be achieved and plan how they will achieve these goals. They work with a clear objective in mind and can see the big picture.

Many people see what needs doing, but the difference is, a leader takes the ACTION required to complete the things that need doing.

A leader may have volunteered for the job, been promoted to this position or inherited the task. Or they may have become so frustrated with the lack of existing leadership, that they are compelled to take charge of a project, just to get it done.

The job of being a leader is bigger than the individual. As well as being responsible for your personal contribution to a project, you are responsible for the development and results of others.

Not all leaders have the title of leader, but the consensus is that they are the person that others look to for leadership and guidance.

Human beings are programmed to work as part of a team and follow a leader. It's how we have survived as a species and how we get things done.

An explosion of skilled leadership in the Middle East, Asia, South America and Africa is building cities, infrastructure and creating completely new business markets faster that at any time in history.

The essential key to any successful business is the quality of their leadership.

The qualities that true leaders display are:

Self-awareness – They know their strengths, weaknesses, capabilities and limitations.

Visionary – They see the bigger picture and are working to achieve something bigger than just a personal gain. They can imagine the end result for everyone involved in a project.

Self-motivated – They don't need others to motivate them, when things get tough they find the resources and energy within themselves to get things done.

Decisive – They make decisions, and know it's sometimes better to make a wrong decision than no decision at all. They recognise that some decisions have to be made quickly, whilst others need more deliberation.

Controlled emotionally – They stay calm and clear-headed and are able to make rational decisions, no matter what is going on around them.

Neutral – They don't get pulled into the drama, gossip and politics around them.

Factual – They work with facts, evidence and data – not hearsay!

Value others – They give feedback on the behaviour of someone, rather than giving comments about that person.

Encouraging – they enjoy helping people believe in their capabilities, developing others to stand on their own feet and become the leaders of the future.

Inspiring – They create genuine energy and enthusiasm in the people they lead. People sense when a leader is not coming from a place of ego, and this results in people wanting to work with that leader, creating a win-win situation.

Skills Action

How many of the above qualities do you already have?

What evidence do you have, from others, that you have those qualities?

For those qualities that you don't yet have, what needs to happen for you to develop them?

We Live In Two Worlds

"Leadership is the art of getting someone else to do something you want done because he wants to do it."
Dwight D. Eisenhower

We do everything twice, once in our inside world and then we take the action to make this happen in the outside world.

Think about it, how did you get dressed this morning? You thought about what you were doing today, and then imagined yourself doing it (your inside world).

When you decided what to wear, you went (in the outside world) to get your clothes and put them on.

It doesn't matter whether you did this just before you rushed out the door today, or spent days planning what to wear, the fact is you did it twice, once in your inside world (also called your imagination) and again in the outside world.

No two people experience the world in the same way. We all have our own perspective of situations based on how we filter information from the external world into our internal world.

Your internal world is unique to you. You create your world by filtering the information from everything you experience in life through your five senses. What you see, feel, hear, taste and smell.

This information is filtered into your brain at speeds beyond what you could possibly imagine. Some of this information you are consciously aware of, however most passes automatically into your unconscious mind.

For you to make sense of the world, you compare every new experience (in your mind) to previous things you have done. You then decide how this fits with your previous experiences, values and beliefs.

Your internal world likes what is familiar, and you edit each new experience to fit with what you already know. This is where you create, what is sometimes called, your 'Map of the World'.

You can only fix problems in your internal world by changing how you think and feel.

For example, this quote from Henry Ford explains this perfectly "Whether **you think you can**, or **you think you can**'t - you're right."

The external world is where other people, events and situations you can see, hear, touch, taste and smell are. It is where our home, office and cars are and where our friends, family and colleagues live.

You can only fix problems in the external world from the outside.

For example if a chair, car or window is broken then you have to either go and get it repaired or replace it with a new one.

Just thinking about it (in your inside world) will not fix something (although plenty of people would like to think that it does!!). Action needs to be taken in the outside world to get something fixed.

True leaders have the ability to step out of their own inside world, and see things from the perspective of someone else.

Skills Action

The following exercise helps you become more conscious about how you experience your internal world.

When you know how you experience your internal world, it's easier to appreciate the different ways that other people experience their internal world.

Think about the front door to your house and point to where you imagine seeing it.

(If you are in your house, then think about another door, maybe your office door.

Notice the detail you get in your mind when you think about this door.

Point to where you see that door.

Is it in front of you or to one side?

Are you looking up at the door or looking down?

Point to where the door handle is.

Point to where the lock is.

What colour is your door?

Imaging opening the door, does it move towards you or away from you?

When you did this, did you actually move your hand toward your door to check?

Are you looking at the door from the inside or outside of your house (or office)?

Point to where the letterbox is (if you have one).

What way does the key turn in the lock?

Turn your key now.

Are your hands turning an imaginary key?

Is there a doorbell or doorknocker?

Did you move to press the doorbell?

How does it sound?

Point to where you hear the sound coming from.

Am I correct is saying that what you are experiencing is not a real live door? You can't physically knock on this door or feel the texture of the surface but you can imagine how your door looks, feels and sounds.

You may even have actually moved your hands to check what way the door opened, and what way the key turned.

We all see, feel and hear our door in our own way. Other people will see their door in their way. Even when two people are imagining the same door, there will be differences in how they do this.

You don't just have this amount of detail when imagining your front door, this is the complexity with which you experience everything you think about, whether it is a memory of a situation that has happened or something you have not done yet.

The R.A.F.T. Model©

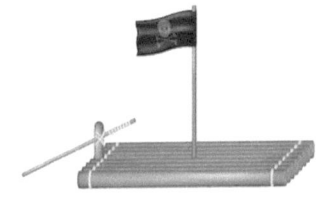

Results

Actions

Feelings

Thoughts

Results and **Actions** are in the Outside World

Feelings and **Thoughts** are in the inside World

Your **R.A.F.T.** moves you from where you are to where you want to be:

- Your **results** are impacted by your actions, feelings and thoughts.

- The **actions** you take (or not!) impact upon your results.

- How you are **feeling** about achieving something impacts upon your results.

- What you are **thinking** or saying to yourself impacts upon your results.

When I was a sales manager, I noticed most of my colleagues, when working with their salespeople, only focused on targets and goals and what people had to do to achieve these targets.

When someone was not performing, the focus was on what could they do more of. How many more calls or appointments could they make? In other words, how much more action is needed.

Very few people asked the questions "how do you feel about achieving your target?" or "when you're thinking about this target, what do you say to yourself?"

These are two powerful questions, because the answers you get give a good indication of what was going on in the inside world of that person.

Asking, "how do you feel about..." is a very specific question. It will give you a totally different answer to "what are you feeling about..."

Here are some real life answers my clients have given me when asked, "How do you feel about this project you are working on?"

"I feel scattered"

"I feel rock solid"

"I feel all over the place"

"I feel I am going round in circles"

"I feel in two minds"

"I feel that it's a done deal"

"I feel sure"

"I feel really confident"

These answers are not describing what we would term emotions, they are literally describing how that person is feeling about the situation you are discussing.

Asking, "what are you saying to yourself" tells you the self-talk or conversation someone is having with themselves. This is also known as your 'internal dialogue'.

Here are some real life answers my clients have given me when asked, "What are you saying to yourself when you think about this project you are working on?"

"I will never get to the end of this"

"I have lost control of this project"

"This is not going to work"

"I am really confident about this"

"I will get this project finished on time"

"I have checked everything"

"I give up"

"I never get to speak to the right people"

"I will find a way round these problems"

These answers let you know how someone is thinking, and the outcome they are expecting to happen. Some of these answers are resourceful and some are not. In each case whatever someone is saying to themselves impacts upon the result they end up getting.

Once you have an insight into someone's inner world, you can help them identify whether what they are thinking and feeling is resourceful or not for achieving their objectives.

If someone is saying to themselves "I will never get this target," and feeling like they are going round in circles," helping them change what they say to themselves and feel differently about the outcome will change the result.

The **R.A.F.T.© Model** will take you through this process step by step:

Skills Action

The steps of the R.A.F.T. Model©

Identify something that did not turn out the way you expected it to – the undesired outcome.

Put this in the **result** box

What actions did you take, or not take, to get this result?

Put this in the **action** box

How did you feel, when you were working towards this result?

Put this in the **feelings** box

What were you thinking and saying to yourself, when you were working towards this result?

Put this in the **thoughts** box

1. Undesired Outcome

Result	Action	Feelings	Thoughts

Repeat the previous steps for something that turned out exactly as you expected it to- the desired outcome.

2. Desired Outcome

Result	Action	Feelings	Thoughts

Compare the tables. How would your result have changed in the first example, if you had thought, felt and done, what you did in the second example?

This tool enables leaders to quickly identify the impact of their thoughts and feelings on their results.

Keeping Your Leadership Styles Clean

"Courage is what it takes to stand up and speak; courage is also what it takes to sit down and listen."
Winston Churchill

Leading others well requires the flexibility to use a variety of leadership styles and make it clear to others which style you are using, and why.

Leading – is having the vision to take your team forward, whilst developing the people within that team to take personal responsibility for their actions – going there first, inspiring others.

Coaching – is facilitating, motivating and encouraging your team members to set specific goals within a specific timeline and for them to take personal responsibility, and the action required to achieve this outcome themselves.

Managing - is controlling and directing your team members according to principles or values that have already been established – managing situations, processes and telling people what to do.

Mentoring – is sharing your knowledge and experience to develop an individual. Passing on your own experience, encouraging and advising

Training – is teaching new skills to others. Helping them become skillful at tasks, processes and systems.

All the above approaches have their place in the business world. Problems can arise when people become confused as to which style you are using.

There is no point in telling someone what to do and then giving them a hard time for not developing themselves. When you do this they are receiving mixed messages. This causes confusion and when someone is confused and don't know what is required of them, they are not productive.

Keep these styles separate

When you are leading or coaching, your job is to encourage others to take responsibility for achieving their objectives. You do this by listening and encouraging someone to think about the different things they can do to achieve their goals.

This is not the right time to 'rescue people' and give them the answers to problems. Doing so prevents people developing themselves, because they will develop the habit of coming to you to solve their problems.

When you are managing people, you are keeping them on track and helping them to keep to systems and processes that are already established. You do this by giving clear instructions of what is required by whom and by when.

When you are mentoring, you talk about your experiences, projects and jobs you have worked on, so that someone can accelerate their learning. You do this by sharing examples and stories of how you dealt with situations in your past, similar to what someone is dealing with now.

When you are training you are teaching new skills, processes and procedures to someone. You do this by clearly identifying the new thing someone is learning, what it will do for them and how it will fit with their job.

One way to help others understand and be clear about the specific leadership style you are using is to refer to the different 'hats' you are wearing.

For example, when I am coaching a client, and want to tell them a story about how someone resolved a similar situation that my client has a problem with, I will say:

"I have a story about that but before I tell you it - hang on a minute, let me take off my coaching hat and put on my mentor hat."

As I say that I actually 'act out' removing a hat a putting on the floor. When I finish I 'act out' picking the hat back up and putting it on.

This way I am giving a visual instruction (the acting out) and auditory instruction (telling them I am taking off my hat) and bringing humour into the coaching situation.

This allows my client to clearly know that I am now sharing possible solutions, as a mentor, rather than coaching them to come up with their own solution.

All the above approaches have their place in the business world and good leaders have the flexibility to move between all five styles depending upon the circumstances.

Skills Action

Write down the different situations you deal with, and which style or styles are the most appropriate for each situation.

Practice the transition from one style to the next. You can use the 'changing hats' technique. Or you may want to develop your own way of letting others know you are moving from one style to another.

When people understand which leadership style you are using, it reduces confusion because they know what is expected of them.

Creating A Leadership Mindset

"Leaders think and talk about the solutions. Followers think and talk about the problems." **Brian Tracy**

A leadership mindset, is when someone looks for different ways to solve a problem rather than focusing on the problem.

There are leaders in companies that thrive, keep positive and focused, even when going through tough times. How are they doing it?

Over the years I have worked with thousands of business leaders, and they tend to fall into two categories.

The first category is the leader who, no matter whether the economy was booming or crashing, is fearful of what was happening. Frightened of losing their job, believing there are no customers for their business and that no one is spending money. They are spending time focusing on the potential problems and all the things that can go wrong. What I call a 'Problem Mindset'.

The second categories is the leader that has never been busier, getting lots of new clients and is excited about all the new opportunities the future presents. They focus on solutions, pre-empting what can go wrong and find ways to overcome possible problems. What I call a 'Solution Mindset'.

So, how do you move from a problem mindset to a solutions mindset?

Asking yourself resourceful questions allows your brain to create more choices to see things in different ways.

As soon as you have more choices, you have movement; even if one of the choices is to walk away, you are no longer 'stuck' in the problem.

Skills Action

Creating a solution 'Mindset'

Your brain is like a wonderful search engine that is compelled to answer any question you ask it. To experience how easy it is to change your way of thinking do the following:

Grab your workbook, a piece of paper and a pen or pencil

1. Choose a problem that you have, at work, that you have not yet resolved.

2. Got it?

3. Ask yourself "why is this a problem?"

4. Write down at least 5 reasons why this is a problem.

5. OK - give your body a shake.

6. Now think of the same situation and this time ask yourself the question "What needs to happen to resolve this situation?"

7. Write down at least 10 ways that this could be resolved. If you get stuck keep asking yourself the question "and what else?"

Stop only when you have at least 10 choices.

Because you now have at least 10 different possible solutions to that situation, you are no longer 'stuck' in that problem.

This exercise teaches you to change your way of thinking, from a problem-focused mindset to a solution-focused mindset.

When you change the questions you ask yourself, your brain will come up with different answers.

The next time you find yourself with a problem to solve, ask yourself the questions "what needs to happen?" and "what else?"

This will give you the choices to resolve this situation, rather than the evidence to confirm it is a problem.

Using Intention To Reduce Meeting Times

"You were born to win, but to be a winner, you must plan to win, prepare to win, and expect to win." **Zig Ziglar**

Knowing the intention of why you are doing something is a valuable leadership skill.

The word intention means, purpose, aim, goal, target, objective and plan. This is an extremely powerful word to use in business.

The job of a leader is to know the overall **intention** of the projects they are responsible for, and drive these projects to completion, by motivating their team to do their job well, and keep to the plan.

People stay focused on a project, when they clearly understand the intention of what they are expected to achieve.

For example, if you want a report sent to you by next Wednesday, it is not useful to just ask someone to send you the report when they have finished it.

Let them know that the intention is to have all the monthly reports completed and submitted to head office by next Friday. To achieve this, all reports need to be completed by Wednesday.

The area where the power of intention becomes really effective is when chairing meetings.

The time wasted in meetings costs companies a fortune. People love to talk, and never more so than when they are in business meetings. Millions of working hours are wasted by unproductive meetings when people go off on different tangents that have nothing to do with the point of the meeting.

The preparation for a productive meeting includes sending out an agenda, letting others know clearly how long the meeting will last, and outcome that you intend to have achieved by the end of the meeting.

It is the responsibility of a leader, when chairing a meeting, to keep focusing people back to the intention of the meeting.

Asking resourceful questions to get the answers that provide solutions, will speed things along.

For example when you ask the question "how are we going to solve this problem?" People tend to focus on the problem first.

When the question is changed to "We have this problem, so what needs to happen for us to resolve it?" People tend to focus first on the solutions.

A great law for you to know about, is **'Parkinson's Law'** (Prof. Cyril Nothcote Parkinson's)

'Work expands so as to fill the time available for its completion'

Whether a meeting has been booked for one hour or five hours, people will finish that meeting, in the time allocated.

I am sure you have attended business meetings that were a total waste of time. There is an agenda, but nobody knows what the purpose or intent of the meeting is, far less the action to be taken as a result of this meeting.

When you count up the cost of man-hours, travel, accommodation and time spent away from the core task of a job, meetings cost companies a lot of money.

Without the intention of what needs to be achieved by the end of that meeting, people relax and wander away from the point. When the objective of the meeting goes off track, the meeting becomes a waste of time.

Imagine going to a meeting that used to take 3 hours with only an agenda and no actionable outcome. Now imagine the same meeting, when you know before the meeting, that the intention is for this meeting to last 40 minutes, and by that time everyone will have achieved a specific outcome.

When people come to a meeting knowing what is expected of them (rather than just attending!!) a sense of urgency is created. When you experience a feeling of urgency, your physiology changes, the brain speeds up and things get done quicker. This creates shorter and more productive meetings.

The leader's job is that of a conductor, after all, you regularly hear people say "Who is conducting this meeting?" Your job is to conduct the meeting and focus people back to the purpose and intention of that meeting.

You can only do this when you have taken the time to clearly set out what you want to achieve in this meeting and by when.

Case History

One of my private clients reduced his monthly managers meetings, from 8 hours to just 3 hours.

When he became Managing Director, the company had a culture of holding monthly Managers' meetings, which could easily go on for eight hours or more.

He quickly identified that his managers expected the meeting to take this time, there was no intention of what was to be achieved, just a list of topics to talk through.

The last topic on the agenda was – any other business!! This would often result in problems being raised, and hours of discussion with no effective outcome.

He changed the format of the meeting by setting a time limit. He stared with 6 hours, and within 3 months, he gradually reduced the time down to 3 hours.

Everyone was sent the outline of the meeting, the time it would take, what the meeting was for and what plan of action would be achieved by the end of that meeting.

He dropped 'any other business' from the agenda, and asked his management team to let him know in advance, of anything else they wanted to cover, that was not on the agenda.

He could then decide, in advance of the meeting, whether to address this topic at that meeting, or move it to another meeting.

The result was his managers developed the habit of attending effective meetings, with a clear intention to leave with a specific plan of action.

The managers then replicated this format of meetings with their own teams, substantially reducing the time wasted in ineffective meetings throughout the whole company.

Skills Action

When you plan future meetings take the following steps.

1. Before the meeting, decide your intention (outcome) and what this meeting will achieve.

2. Set the time you will have achieved this by, for example 30 minutes, 1 hour etc.

3. Invite only the people who need to attend.

4. Let everyone who is attending the meeting know the subject of the meeting, what they have to bring with them, the time the

meeting will take, the intention of what this meeting will achieve and what action will follow.

For example, the quarterly sales meeting will start at 11am finish at 1pm. Please bring your figures from quarter one to review. We will review where the company is to date. You will leave with your plan of action to achieve your objectives for quarter two.

5. Construct your questions to get the answers you want, ask people "what needs to happen to resolve this?" " How specifically will you achieve this?"

6. **<u>Keep</u>** to the time set.

7. Keep focusing people back to the intention of the meeting.

Verbal and non-verbal communication

"To handle yourself, use your head; to handle others, use your heart."
Eleanor Roosevelt

Only 20% to 30% of your communication is verbal (earlier studies stated it was only 7%). That means that 70% to 80% of how you communicate is by the tone of your voice and body movement.

Do you know how your voice sounds to others? Very few leaders I work with can answer 'yes' to this question. Those that do know what they sound like, often don't like to listen to themselves speak!

If you don't know how your voice sounds or don't like hearing yourself speak, how can you expect others to enjoy listening to you?

How do you look to others? Do you come across as confident and sure about what you are saying, or do you come across as fidgety and unsure.

At one of my senior director trainings, a gentleman, when asked what he wanted to achieve at the training, said (in a dull, flat voice, whilst looking at the floor) "I want to inspire and motivate my team."

I asked him if he would be inspired and motivated, if someone spoke to him in the same tone of voice whilst looking at the floor, and he said no!

Knowing yourself as others see and hear you helps you to hone your leadership skills.

Get to know how your voice sounds to others, because your voice is a very powerful leadership tool.

Think of the great leaders who inspire you, how do they look and sound? How do they convey being passionate about something?

If they have something serious to say, how do they still manage to inspire and motivate others, even when delivering a tough message?

When talking about something that is exciting, look and sound excited! If you are passionate about what you are saying, look and sound passionate.

When you are excited or passionate about something, it's infectious and creates good feelings in others.

For years, I have been teaching people to put a giggle into their voice when saying things to energise others. I don't mean actually giggle when you are talking. I mean create the feeling of having a giggle at the back of your throat. When you talk over that 'giggle' feeling you create a great energy, which other people pick up on.

When you have something challenging to say, keep your voice neutral and matter of fact. Even if you feel depressed about giving this information, it is not resourceful to pass on your depression through your voice and body posture to others.

The role of a leader is sometimes to give tough news. People want to know the truth, so stick to the facts, keep to the point and keep your voice strong.

Skills Action

To see how you look and hear what you sound like, record yourself on video. Video cameras are available on all smart phones, and if you don't have one, borrow one!!

Part One: Film yourself working through the following instructions.

Choose a message you would give to others. For example. "I am delighted that you took the time to finish your report early" Say this sentence by moving your voice to speak.

From your nose.

From your lips.

From your throat.

From your chest.

From your stomach.

Notice how the message comes across (including the volume and tone of your voice) when you say the same thing, from different parts of your body.

When you speak from your throat, it creates a sound of tightness and uncertainty, about what you are saying. You may just be nervous, but to the listener it looks and sounds as if you are not sure about your subject.

Speaking from your stomach creates a sense of ease for the listener, because it looks and sounds as if you are really sure, and confident about the subject you are talking about.

Part Two: Film yourself, giving the same message as the previous exercise, and say the message while imagining the following:

You are fed up.

You are excited.

You talk in a controlled, neutral manner.

You are feeling mischievous.

You are strong.

You are quietly confident.

You are powerful.

Notice how different a message comes across when you change the feelings behind the message.

Become comfortable with how you look and sound when talking to others. Pay attention to how your tonality and body posture is affecting the message you are giving.

Leading Others

"Leadership is not about titles, positions or flowcharts. It is about one life influencing another." **John C. Maxwell**

Part of leading others, is the ability to believe that you can achieve something, even if you don't know how you are going to get there yet!

People quickly spot hesitation in leaders. When people pick up that their leader is not sure about a project or task, it is often seen as a sign of weakness. When people suspect that their leader is weak, team dynamics crumble.

Leaders are people who stand up and take responsibility. Not everyone wants to be a leader. A simple way identify who wants to lead a project and who wants to follow is just ask a group of people "'Who wants to take charge of this project?" Watch and listen to what happens.

Maybe 2% of people will say "I will" and the rest will put on (what I call) their 'invisibility cloaks'. They won't look at you, in the hope that if they don't look at you, you won't see them and pick them to lead!!

This is a non-verbal signal that they have no desire to challenge the leadership position. If most people do not want to lead, that means that leaders are a rare breed, so how does knowing this help you be a better leader?

For a start, it means that if you are leading then you have followers (which is the first criteria of being a leader). It also means that by assuming the leadership position you become personally responsible for leading others.

You now have the choice of doing the job badly or well. If you only want the 'job title' of a leader and not the responsibility, then you are not a true leader.

Many people in leadership positions have had no formal training in leading others. Very often they are promoted into a position of leadership because they are good at the job they do.

The book The Peter Principle by Laurence J Peter and Raymond Hull (published in 1969 by William Morrow and Co) offers the theory.

'Employees within an organisation will advance to their highest level of competence and then be promoted to, and remain at a level at which they are incompetent.'

Although this book was published in 1969 the message still holds true in business today.

Just because someone is good at a specific job does not mean that they will become a good leader. Leadership is a skill that requires continuous development.

All good leaders, whether they are natural leaders or not, know the importance of being one-step ahead of the game. They know the capabilities of the people in their team(s) well, and know who can do what. They have the flexibility to know when people need gentle handling, or a tougher approach.

One of the biggest mistakes many business leaders make, is expecting other people to do things in the same way that they do. They have not yet grasped the concept that no two human beings are the same.

We all create our own realities based on our unique life experiences. What we experience shapes our beliefs and what we think, feel and do creates the results in our lives.

Often leaders can forget the purpose of being a leader is - to motivate and inspire a group of individuals with their own unique resources to all work together to achieve an end result.

When a team is badly led, and the individual strengths and styles of the people in that team are not recognised and valued, people can quickly become highly stressed, de-motivated and un-resourceful. This can lead to increased absenteeism, time wasting and increased costs.

A well-led team is a highly creative, flexible and dynamic force made up of individual personalities who use their own resources to achieve set results in the quickest and most efficient way possible.

Skills Action

Get to know the qualities and capabilities of the people you either lead or work with.

Identify what qualities you require to develop in yourself, to become an even better leader.

Knowing yourself

"Leadership is a series of behaviors rather than a role for heroes."
Margaret Wheatley

True leaders know that the responsibility of being a leader is bigger than them. They are only able to lead others well when they know themselves and 'think about their thinking'.

This book has covered different aspects of communication and behavior from the leadership point of view. To work well with others it is vital that you know how you are perceived as a leader.

Skills Action

Answer the following questions as honestly as you can to become more aware about knowing yourself and your ability to lead others.

1. How do you lead (or would want to lead) others?

2. How do others see you?

3. How do you sound to others?

4. What evidence do you have that you are a good leader?

Now go and ask the people you work with how you come across as a leader, or, if you don't lead others yet, how they think you would come across as a leader.

Be subtle and curious. This is not an interrogation or a 'build your own fan club' exercise! Encourage people to tell you (constructively) and honestly, things that you may not know about yourself.

Often, when doing this exercise people do not like what they hear. They can be uncomfortable with praise or only choose to perceive what they hear as a negative.

Use this as an opportunity to step away from your emotions and stop making judgments.

This exercise is about getting information about how you come across to others, and using this information to become even better at what you do.

Roundup

"Don't tell people how to do things, tell them what to do and let them surprise you with their results."
George S. Patton Jr.

The topics covered in this book are just a few of the many ways you can get to know yourself better as a leader. There is no 'perfect' way to lead people. You will, over time, develop a style that is perfect for you.

Working through the Skills Actions in this book will help you become more aware of yourself and how you come across to others.

When you are familiar with using the R.A.F.T. Model, creating a leadership mindset and intention to reduce meeting times, you can use these exercises to develop others.

All the successful leaders I have met, without exception, believe in the principle of life-long learning. They continue to improve themselves and take time to reflect on their performance. They seek feedback and evidence to measure how well they lead others. They are willing to take on new challenges and stretch themselves to be the best they can be.

Leading is not about telling, it is about listening, observing and having a good grip on situations. It is about understanding others and developing them to be much better than they personally think they can be. It is taking personal responsibility to stand up and admit when things have gone wrong and celebrating with others when things have been successful.

Keep developing yourself and you will become the leader you always wanted to be.

Here is to your continued success!

Fiona Campbell

About The Author

Fiona Campbell helps senior executives enhance their communication skills for developing their key people, growing their business and creating a great place for people to work.

She is an Executive Coach, internationally licensed NLP Business Coach Trainer for the Society of NLP and was a member of the team who assisted Paul McKenna and Richard Bandler on their NLP training courses in London for over eight years.

In 2001 Fiona progressed to coaching and training after a highly successful corporate sales career. In her private practice she coaches and supports CEO's and Company Directors to clarify their vision and achieve their goals.

Her passion is helping leaders inspire, develop and motivate others and create a fun, healthy and highly productive working environment.

Find her other books at
http://www.amazon.com/Fiona-Campbell/e/B007NFI9N0

www.ingramcontent.com/pod-product-compliance
Lightning Source LLC
Chambersburg PA
CBHW020710180526
45163CB00008B/3015